THE **TESTING** SERIES

FIREFIGHTER APPLICATION FORM **QUESTIONS & ANSWERS**

Orders: Please contact How2become Ltd, Suite 2, 50 Churchill Square Business Centre, Kings Hill, Kent ME19 4YU. You can also order via the e mail address info@how2become.co.uk and at Gardners.com.

ISBN: 9781907558696

First published 2012

Typeset for How2become Ltd by Molly Hill, Canada.

Printed in Great Britain for How2become Ltd by Bell & Bain Ltd, 303 Burnfield Road, Thornliebank, Glasgow G46 7UQ.

INTRODUCTION

Welcome to Firefighter Application Form Questions & Answers. This guide has been designed to help you pass the initial stage of the tough firefighter selection process.

The author of this guide, Richard McMunn, spent over 16 years in the UK Fire Service. He worked at many different fire stations at every position up to Station Manager, and he has also sat on numerous interview panels assessing potential candidates to join the job. You will find his advice invaluable and inspiring in your pursuit to joining what is probably one of the most exciting careers available.

Whilst the selection process to join the Fire Service is highly competitive, there are a number of things you can do in order to improve your chances of success, and they are all contained within this guide.

The way to prepare for a job in the Fire Service is to embark on a programme of 'in depth' preparation, and this guide will show you exactly how to do that.

If you need any help with motivation, getting fit or further interview help and advice, then we offer a wide range of products to assist you. These are all available through our online shop **www.how2become.co.uk**.

We also run a 1-day intensive Firefighter Course. Details of the course are available at the website

WWW.FIREFIGHTERCOURSE.CO.UK

Once again, thank you for your custom and we wish you every success in your pursuit to becoming a firefighter. Work hard, stay focused and be what you want...

Best wishes,

The how2become team

The How2become Team

PREFACE BY AUTHOR RICHARD MCMUNN

I joined the Fire Service on January the 25th 1993 after completing four years in the Fleet Air Arm branch of the Royal Navy. In the build-up to joining the Fire Service I embarked on a comprehensive training programme that would see me pass the selection process with relative ease. The reason why I passed the selection process with ease was solely due to the preparation and hard work that I had put in during the build-up.

I have always been a great believer in preparation. Preparation was my key to success and it is also yours. Without the right level of preparation you will be setting out on the route to failure. The Fire Service is very hard to join but if you follow the steps that I have compiled within this guide then you will increase your chances of success dramatically.

Remember, you are learning how to be a successful candidate, not a successful firefighter!

The Fire Service has changed a great deal over the past few years and even more so in how it assesses potential candidates for firefighter positions. When I joined in 1993, it helped if you were 6ft tall, built like a mountain and from a military background. Things have certainly changed since then, and rightly so. Yes, the Fire Service still needs people of that calibre but it also needs people who represent the community in which it serves.

It needs people from different backgrounds, different cultures, different ages, different sexual orientations and different genders. Basically, the community in which we live is diverse in nature, and therefore so should the Fire Service if it is to provide a high level of service the public deserve. Most of us will thankfully go through life never having to call upon the Fire Service. Those who do call on the Fire Service expect their firefighters to be physically fit, professional and highly competent in their role.

During my time in the Fire Service I attended hundreds of different incidents ranging from property fires, road traffic collisions, chemical incidents, ship fires and even rail accidents. During every single one of them I gave my all, and so did my colleagues. During your time in the Fire Service you will experience many highs and many lows. The highs will come from your ability and influence to save a person's life and naturally the lows will come from the people whom you sadly could not help. How you handle the low points of your career is crucial. Fortunately, you will experience an amazing level of comradeship during your career that is extremely rare and is not normally found in other jobs or professions. It is this high level of comradeship that will get you through the low points.

The men and women of the UK Fire Service carry out an amazing job. They are there to protect the community in which they serve and they do that job with great pride, passion and very high levels of professionalism and commitment. They are to be congratulated for the service they provide.

Before you apply to join the Fire Service, you need to be fully confident that you too are capable of providing that same level of service. If you think you can do it, and you can rise to the challenge, then you just might be the type of person the Fire Service is looking for.

As you progress through this application form guide you will notice that the qualities required to be a firefighter are a common theme. You must learn these qualities, and also be able to demonstrate throughout the selection process that you can meet them, if you are to have any chance of successfully passing the selection process.

I wish you all the very best in your pursuit to becoming a firefighter.

Richard McMunn

P.S. Attend my 1-Day Fireifghter course at www.firefightercourse.co.uk.

ABOUT THE FIREFIGHTER APPLICATION FORM

IMPORTANT DISCLAIMER

Within this guide I have provided you with guidance to help you complete the firefighter application form. Please note that the information provided within this guide is for guidance purposes only. I have provided you with sample responses to some of the questions you may encounter on the application form. These sample responses are for guidance purposes only. It is important to remember that the responses you provide should be based solely on your own individual skills and experiences.

The application form is one of the first stages of the firefighter selection process and it is probably the hardest to get through. You will be applying along with many hundreds of other applicants and therefore your application form needs to be outstanding.

Before we move on to how you should consider completing the form, read the following two important notes:

1. Firefighters do not generally retire before their determined retirement date. The reason for this is because it is an exceptional job. Fire Services rarely advertise firefighter posts, so the competition is very

fierce when firefighter vacancies do eventually become available. Therefore your application needs to be very good.

2. Picture the scene – a Fire Service assessor has been marking application forms for the last two weeks. It is late Friday afternoon and they come across your application form. Your application form is hard to read, full of grammar errors and is incomplete in a number of sections. Do you think the form will get through? The answer is no.

It is crucial that your application form is concise, easy to read, neat, and completed in **all** the relevant sections. Take your time to complete a solid application. If you have the time, spend a week completing the form and answer the assessable questions in draft first before committing pen to paper. If you are completing an online application then complete your responses in draft first using notepad or a similar tool.

Whenever I prepare for something in life I always formulate a 'plan'. Let's take a look at how I would personally plan/prepare for the firefighter application form.

- I will make sure that I read all of the information contained within the guidance notes before I start to complete the application form. I will also highlight the key areas within the guidance notes that I must follow. If I do not follow the guidance notes carefully then my application may be rejected.
- When writing my application I will make sure that it is easy to read, concise and that it answers the questions exactly as required. It is my job to make the application form easy to mark. If the assessor has been marking scores of applications, then I want to make it easy for them.

When completing your application form keep a copy of the above points next to you so that they act as an important reminder.

PRE-APPLICATION CHECKLIST

You may find that the firefighter application form includes a pre-application checklist. This is quite straightforward to complete and usually involves a tick box section.

The first checklist involves questions such as:

ARE YOU PREPARED TO:

- Work at height?
- Work in enclosed spaces?
- Work outdoors?
- Get wet during your work?
- Get hot / cold whilst working?
- Carry heavy equipment?
- Work unsociable hours?
- Work in situations where you may see blood, seriously injured, or dead people?
- Deal sensitively with people in difficult situations?
- Work with a diverse range of people (e.g. of different ages, ethnic backgrounds etc)?

Those candidates who tick no to any of the above questions are unlikely to proceed to the next stages of the selection process.

The next part of the form is usually the personal details section. Once again this is straightforward to complete. The only advice that I can provide you with here is to be honest. Any false or misleading information may deem your application void.

ASSESSMENT OF PERSONAL QUALITIES

This section is designed to assess your personal qualities and attributes against that of a firefighter. When responding to the questions in this section you can draw on any of your experiences either from your home life, leisure activities, work (paid or unpaid) or education.

The questions are usually divided into 3 parts as follows:

- What you did.
- Why you did it.
- What happened as a result of your actions?

You may find that these questions are worded in a different manner to the above; however, if they are different, they will be similar.

ADVICE ON ANSWERING THE QUESTIONS THAT RELATE TO THE PERSONAL QUALITIES

- Take your time when completing the questions and follow the advice contained within the section. Remember the 'plan'!
- Remember that you are competing against many other candidates, so take your time to get it right.
- Use recent examples when responding to the questions.
- Try to use 'keywords' in your responses to the questions that relate to the personal qualities and attributes (PQAs) that are being assessed.
- Make sure that you answer EVERY question.
- Do not go over the allocated 'word count'.
- Be specific about one particular scenario.
- Write down your answers in rough first.
- Remember to photocopy the application form before sending it off. You may need to refer to it before attending your interview.
- Make sure your handwriting is neat and legible. Get someone to read it back to you once completed. If they struggle to read any words or sentences then so will the person assessing your form.
- Read the completed application form carefully before sending it off. The competition is fierce and you need to ensure that you stay ahead of the other candidates, most of who will not be as prepared as you.

I have now provided a number of sample questions and answers to assist you in responding to the PQA based questions.

SAMPLE QUESTION 1

Describe a situation where you have worked with people who are different from you in relation to age, background or gender.

This question has been designed to assess your ability to work with others regardless of their background, age or gender. The Fire Service is a diverse workforce and therefore it requires people who have the ability to work in such an environment.

When answering this question, try to think of an occasion when you have worked with people who are different from you in terms of age, background or gender.

Remember to be specific in your response, relating it to a particular situation.

Do not be generic in your response. An example of a generic response would be – *'I am comfortable working with people from different backgrounds and have done this on many occasions'.* This type of response is not specific and does not relate to a situation. Make sure you have a copy of the firefighter PQAs next to you when responding to this question and try to include keywords in your response.

Now take a look at the following example response before using a blank sheet of paper to construct your own response based on your experiences.

QUESTION 1 – SAMPLE RESPONSE ONLY

Describe a situation where you have worked with people who are different from you in relation to age, background or gender. (Maximum of 150 words)

WHAT DID YOU DO?

Whilst working in my current role as a sales assistant I was tasked with working with a new member of the team. The lady had just started working with us and was unfamiliar with the role. She was from a different background and appeared to be very nervous. I tried to comfort her and told her that I was there to support her through her first few working days and help her get her feet under the table.

WHY?

I fully understood how she must have felt. It was important that I supported her and helped her through her first few days at work. We are there to help each other regardless of age, background or gender.

WHAT HAPPENED AS A RESULT?

The lady settled into work well and is now very happy in her role. We have been working together for 3 months and have built up a close professional and personal relationship.

SAMPLE QUESTION 2

Describe a situation where you have worked closely with other people as part of a team.

As a firefighter, having the ability to build working relationships with your colleagues is very important. After all, they are relying on you to be supportive when you attend operational incidents and also during other tasks that you will be required to perform as a team.

This question is designed to see whether you have the ability to fulfil that role.

Remember again to be specific about a particular situation and avoid the pitfall of being too generic.

Try to think of a situation when you have worked as part of a team, maybe to achieve a common goal or task. The following is a sample response to this question. Read it and take notes before using a blank sheet of paper to create your own response.

QUESTION 2 – SAMPLE RESPONSE

Describe a situation where you have worked closely with other people as part of a team.

WHAT DID YOU DO?

I currently play football for a local Sunday team and we were in fear of relegation to a lower league. I offered to help the team out by arranging and coordinating an extra training session on a weekday evening so that we could look for ways to improve our skills.

WHY?

I felt that the team needed support and encouragement. We all needed to work together to improve our skills. I knew that unless the team pulled together and began to work closely as a unit we would be relegated.

WHAT HAPPENED AS A RESULT?

We all met up for the extra training sessions and worked on our skills and fitness whilst supporting and helping each other. I helped a team-mate to work on his fitness levels by running 3 miles with him every session. At the end of the season we managed to avoid relegation due to the combined team effort.

SAMPLE QUESTION 3

Describe a situation where you have taken steps to improve your skills and/or learn new things.

As a firefighter you will constantly be learning new things. Amongst other things, you will learn new and amended operational procedures, how to operate operational equipment and you will also attend courses to learn new skills. Therefore, the Fire Service wants to know that you already have the potential to improve your skills and learn new things.

When answering this question, try to think of an example where you have learnt something new. This may be through your working life, at home or in your leisure time. There are probably many experiences that you can draw from so take the time to think of a suitable response.

I have now provided a sample response to help you. Once you have read it, use a blank sheet of paper to create your own.

QUESTION 3 – SAMPLE RESPONSE

Describe a situation where you have taken steps to improve your skills and/or learn new things.

WHAT DID YOU DO?

Approximately three months ago I asked my line manager if I could attend a two-day customer care skills course. I work as a sales assistant for a large leisure retail outlet. The course was quite in depth and whilst on it I learnt new skills including how to provide a better level of service.

WHY?

I wanted to improve my skills in customer care. I am always looking for ways to improve my knowledge and learn new things. I also felt that by attending the course I would be improving the level of service that our customers receive.

WHAT WAS THE RESULT?

I successfully passed the course and I received a qualification in customer care skills. I feel more confident in my abilities and feel more qualified to perform my role. As a result of the course I have also improved the level of service to the customer.

SAMPLE QUESTION 4

Describe a situation where you have had to remain calm and controlled in a stressful situation.

Obviously as a firefighter the public depend on you to stay calm, confident and in control during stressful situations. This skill is crucial to the role of an operational firefighter.

When responding to this question, think of an occasion where you have had to stay calm and in control. This does not necessarily have to be in a work situation but it may be during leisure time or at home. Be careful not to answer this question generically. Focus on a particular situation that you encountered recently.

Again, I have provided you with a sample response to this question. Once you have read it, use a blank sheet of paper to construct your own.

QUESTION 4 – SAMPLE RESPONSE

Describe a situation where you have had to remain calm and controlled in a stressful situation.

WHAT DID YOU DO?

Whilst driving home from work I came across a road accident. I parked safely and went over to see if I could help. An elderly lady was in one of the cars suffering from shock. I remained calm and dialled 999 asking for the Police and Ambulance services. Once I had done this I then gave basic First Aid to the lady and ensured that the scene was safe.

WHY?

When I arrived people were starting to panic so I knew that somebody needed to take control of the situation. By remaining calm and confident I was able to get help for the lady.

WHAT HAPPENED AS A RESULT?

Within a few minutes the services arrived and the lady was taken to hospital. The Police then took some details of my actions and thanked me for my calm approach and for making the scene safe.

SAMPLE QUESTION 5

Describe a situation where you have had to work on your own in accordance with guidelines.

Having the ability to work unsupervised, following strict procedural guidance, is an essential element of the firefighter's role.

During operational incidents you will be under the authority of a supervisory manager. However, there will often be times when you have to work on your own unsupervised, and the Fire Service needs people who are capable of carrying out such tasks.

When answering this question, try to think of an occasion when you have worked on your own following specific guidelines. Once again, ensure that you are specific about a particular situation and avoid being too generic.

The following is a sample response to this question. Read it and take notes before using a blank sheet of paper to create your own response.

QUESTION 5 – SAMPLE RESPONSE

Describe a situation where you have had to work on your own in accordance with guidelines.

WHAT DID YOU DO?

Whilst working in my current role as a gas engineer I was tasked with fitting a new boiler to a domestic property in a safe and effective manner. I carried out this work unsupervised and was relied upon to follow strict procedural and safety guidelines.

WHY?

If I did not follow the procedural guidance that I received during my training then I would be putting lives at risk. I must ensure that I carry out my work responsibly and follow all safety procedures to ensure that my work is carried out in accordance with my company's policies.

WHAT HAPPENED AS A RESULT?

The boiler was fitted to the required standard in accordance with the relevant British Standard and all safety procedures were followed. The customer was satisfied with my work and I was happy that I carried out my duties responsibly and in a competent manner.

SAMPLE QUESTION 6

Describe a situation where you have had to change the way you do something following a change imposed by someone in authority.

The Fire Service is constantly looking for ways to modernise, develop and improve. In order for it to complete its modernisation agenda, it requires its employees to be adaptable to change. As a firefighter you will be required to embrace change and actively support it.

When answering this question, try to think of a specific situation, either at work, home or through your leisure activities, where a change has been imposed by someone in authority.

Take a look at the following sample response to this question.

Once you have read it and taken notes, use a blank sheet of paper to construct your own individual answer based on your own experiences.

QUESTION 6 – SAMPLE RESPONSE

Describe a situation where you have had to change the way you do something following a change imposed by someone in authority.

WHAT DID YOU DO?

Whilst working in my current job as a recruitment consultant, my manager wanted to restructure the office and change everyone's roles and responsibilities. The company was performing well but I looked upon this as an opportunity to see if we could improve even further. I fully supported my manager and offered to assist him in the process of change.

WHY?

Change and continuous improvement is important if an organisation is going to keep on top of its game. I embrace change and look at it as a positive thing.

WHAT HAPPENED AS A RESULT?

After approximately 3 months everybody was settled in their new roles. The change had been a success and our end of quarter figures were on the increase. I now also knew a lot more about the organisation than I had previously as a direct result of trying new and different things in the office. The team now works better together.

The next part of the application form may involve additional questions. The following three questions are provided as an example of what you could be required to respond to:

- Why would you be good in the role of a firefighter?
- What skills or experience do you have that you believe are relevant to the role of a firefighter?
- What have you done to find out about what firefighters do?

When answering these three questions, try to think about what the firefighter's role involves. Don't just mention the operational aspect of the role but remember the important sides of Community Fire Safety, reducing fires and risk, and also training. The skills required to become a firefighter are many and varied.

Make sure you visit the website of the Fire Service that you are applying to join. Visit a fire station and ask the local firefighters what they do and what their role involves.

I have now provided sample responses to these three questions. Remember to base your answers on your own experiences.

QUESTION – SAMPLE RESPONSE

Why would you be good in the role of a firefighter?

I believe that I have the necessary skills and attributes to become a competent firefighter. I am a caring and confident person who very much enjoys working with other people of all ages and backgrounds.

I understand that the Fire Service is a continually changing environment. I always embrace change and have experienced it on numerous occasions in my current job. I enjoy working in the community and have experience of working in voluntary organisations and diverse workforces. I enjoy learning new skills and I am always professional in my approach to work. Working in the Fire Service is a customer-focused role and I understand that preventing fires is just as important as responding to them.

I am a reliable, physically fit and dedicated person and believe I would be a valuable asset to the Fire and Rescue Service.

QUESTION – SAMPLE RESPONSE

What skills or experience do you have that you believe are relevant to the role of a firefighter?

I have many years' experience of working in a customer-focused environment where a commitment to excellence is essential.

Within my current role I have a track record for providing a consistent and high level of service. I have sound communication skills and have experience of working in a close team environment where everybody relies on each other to get the job done.

In my current role I am required to work under pressurised conditions and I often work unsupervised. I am an extremely practical person who takes the time to learn new skills and have demonstrated this through attending and successfully passing the Duke of Edinburgh's Award. I have good problem-solving skills, which have been gained through my work as a shop manager.

I have a qualification in Health and Safety and I am conversant in current safe working practices including a good understanding of the risk assessment process.

QUESTION – SAMPLE RESPONSE

What have you done to find out about what firefighters do?

I have taken the time to visit the Fire Service's website and fully understand that the firefighter's role is varied and complex.

I have read the Fire Authority's Community Plan and understand that Community Fire Safety, Home Fire Safety Checks and ongoing fire reduction strategies are integral to the firefighter's work. I have also read the Integrated Risk Management Plan for the Fire Service and understand that there is a three-year plan to look at ways to improve the service.

I have taken the time to read and study the current Race Equality Scheme and understand how important this is to the Fire Service.

Finally, I recently visited the local fire station and spent an hour with the firefighters discussing their job, the equipment they use, the working day and their training.

In the next section of the guide I have provided you with lots of sample application form questions and answers to help you during your preparation.

SAMPLE FIREFIGHTER APPLICATION FORM QUESTIONS AND ANSWERS

DISCLAIMER: the responses that are contained within this guide are not to be copied or duplicated in any manner; they are for illustration and guidance purposes only. It is vital that you complete your own form using answers to the questions that are based on your own unique and individual circumstances. All characters, incidents and situations appearing in this work are fictitious.

WORKING WITH OTHERS

WORKING WITH OTHERS EXAMPLE

Describe a situation when you have had to work with others to complete a task: What was the situation? What was your role? What was the outcome?

On my Public Service HND my lecturer made me team leader of a team of three. We were asked to research leadership theorist, and motivational styles.

I introduced myself and got everyone talking about themselves. We discussed the objectives and I thought it was better to delegate jobs to each other and asked everyone to exchange telephone numbers. I took it upon myself to supply everyone with books from the library corresponding with everyone's task. I also took notes of all meetings, so that we all could remember what we had already done.

One evening a team member sent me a message as he had lost his assignment brief and was struggling. As he did not have any credit and I knew he had dyslexia, I called him and discussed the issues.

I took an active and friendly approach towards the team as I wanted everyone to feel they were contributing to the final goal. I felt communication was important for us staying on track.

We finished our work on time and presented our findings to the class. We were awarded a very high grade. By the end we bonded well and frequently work together as a team.

WORKING WITH OTHERS EXAMPLE

Describe a situation when you have had to work with others to complete a task: What was the situation? What was your role? What was the outcome?

Whilst working at a restaurant as a waiter there was a private booking for 1,500 people. The guests each had a three course meal and any drinks they wished for from the bar throughout the night. We had a team of waiters, bartenders and managers on shift, so we needed to work as a team, prioritise tasks and help our colleges in order to complete the task.

My role was to serve drinks working as a team member with four other bartenders, two of which were inexperienced. We worked efficiently as a team serving guests, clearing up glasses and stocking up the fridges when we were running low. I assisted the inexperienced colleagues by communicating with them and supporting them whenever they needed assistance. During periods where we were not busy I would help the waiters clear up their tables, as well as run soft drinks for the chefs, who were working non-stop in the hot kitchen.

The event ran very smoothly and the guests wrote a letter of gratitude to our Area Manager. The inexperienced team members felt more comfortable in their roles having been able to ask for help on the night and the event's success boosted team moral.

WORKING WITH OTHERS EXAMPLE

Describe a situation when you have had to work with others to complete a task: What was the situation? What was your role? What was the outcome?

I work as a volunteer for a Flying Club. It became apparent that there was inadequate fire and rescue cover for weekend activities on the airfield. There is an essential requirement that there needs to be a minimum of two firefighters per rota to ensure that all activities on the airfield can still take place.

Upon hearing about this situation, I offered to cover this staffing dilemma where I was required to develop a rapport with a member of staff I had never worked with.

By offering to provide the required level of cover, my flexibility ensured that the airfield was able to operate as expected for it would have closed otherwise. I was also able to demonstrate my team skills by working with another individual and helping out in a difficult situation.

WORKING WITH OTHERS EXAMPLE

Describe a situation when you have had to work with others to complete a task: What was the situation? What was your role? What was the outcome?

During my Breathing Apparatus course, one task was to search and rescue on the left hand wall. It was my turn to be number 1 and to lead my number 2 into the building to retrieve any casualties inside. Before we went in, my number 2 and I talked through what our task was and the necessary procedures to follow (leg sweeps; arm sweeps; checking for doors, low openings, landmarks etc; and personal protection).

We encouraged each other while waiting to be instructed to go “Under air”. When we were told to get under air, we did. We checked each other’s PPE before entry. Immediately after entry, I began finding my way through the building while my number 2 searched off me. I gave clear instructions to my partner throughout the task about our location and progress through the building.

On a previous Breathing Apparatus task, my air was lasting longer than my partners. Therefore, I ensured to check my pressure gauge and my partner’s at regular intervals to judge the time we had left. As a team, we found an adult casualty and we both worked together to get the casualty out as quickly and safely as possible.

WORKING WITH OTHERS EXAMPLE

Describe a situation when you have had to work with others to complete a task: What was the situation? What was your role? What was the outcome?

In November last year, two colleagues and I were tasked with carrying out a rewire on a large property over a seven day period. After two days on the job I received a call from my manager telling me that the job was now being cut to five days due to availability issues with staff for the following week. I told my manager that this wouldn't be a problem and that we would pull together as a team in order to get the job completed on time.

I facilitated a plan of action and started by consulting my colleagues to ascertain whether they would be able to work extra hours into the evenings in order to complete the job on time and I cleared this with the customer. I also started early each day in order to plan our routes for running cables whilst causing minimal damage to the property. This would ensure everyone was aware of what had to be done each day whilst managing time effectively.

We were able to complete the job on time by showing commitment, building a rapport and teamwork. The customer was delighted that the work was completed early and to a high standard.

COMMITMENT TO DIVERSITY AND INTEGRITY

COMMITMENT TO DIVERSITY AND INTEGRITY EXAMPLE

Describe a situation when you have worked with a range of people from different communities/equality groups: What was the situation? What were your considerations? What actions did you take to overcome any challenges?

Whilst replenishing stock at work, I noticed a lady in a wheelchair had got stuck. There was already a shop assistant there but he felt uncomfortable and was too busy to deal with the situation. I volunteered to assist the customer by taking her shopping; informing her of the prices; giving her recommendations whilst chatting to her. I then opened a pay-desk and helped her pack. I made sure she left the store safely. I wanted her to be as comfortable by ensuring she did not have to lift, reach or wait in any queues.

I wanted to help as she was finding shopping difficult and I knew the other assistant would have treated her as a chore. Whilst chatting, I found she had a stroke and lost the ability to speak properly with many other basic functions. I believe my previous experiences with elderly and disabled people, had made shopping more pleasurable.

As a result she felt valued, and shopping had changed from a negative to a positive and comfortable experience. She has returned many times. I had also lived up to the store's values of: acting responsibly for our communities and to be first to meet their needs.

COMMITMENT TO DIVERSITY AND INTEGRITY EXAMPLE

Describe a situation when you have worked with a range of people from different communities/equality groups: What was the situation? What were your considerations? What actions did you take to overcome any challenges?

I was working at a restaurant and noticed a divide between the waiters and kitchen staff. Most of the kitchen staff were older than their waiter colleagues and had migrated from India. There was very little interaction between the kitchen and waiter staff colleagues.

My initial considerations were to ensure that the kitchen staff felt comfortable and that they could also speak to me and the waiters if they needed help or assistance. I consider an awareness and respect of others backgrounds to be important in the workplace. I also believe that communication between colleagues within a workplace is essential to achieve the best possible results and create a good working environment, regardless of individual differences.

To overcome the challenges I introduced myself to all the kitchen staff members and learnt their names. I also encouraged the other waiters to communicate with their kitchen colleagues. Following my actions and my awareness of the barriers that existed, communication improved and the workplace is now a more efficient and happier working environment.

COMMITMENT TO DIVERSITY AND INTEGRITY EXAMPLE

Describe a situation when you have worked with a range of people from different communities/equality groups: What was the situation? What were your considerations? What actions did you take to overcome any challenges?

In my previous role as a cadet instructor in St John Ambulance, I was required to assist with training the cadets in the use of radio equipment to prepare them for the various duties they were expected to attend. The group consisted of young people aged between twelve and seventeen and different ethnicities.

I played the role of ensuring respect and trust developed within the group, as this made it easier for them to work together effectively and acquire the skills and knowledge required to operate the radio equipment. I helped with the process of building working relationships within the group so that they were comfortable with working across a wide age gap.

Following my actions the group felt supported, comfortable and confident throughout the six sessions. Nobody in the team felt different or excluded because of age or ethnicity and the feedback I received was positive.

COMMITMENT TO DIVERSITY AND INTEGRITY EXAMPLE

Describe a situation when you have worked with a range of people from different communities/equality groups: What was the situation? What were your considerations? What actions did you take to overcome any challenges?

One day we got a call out to a wheelie bin fire outside a house in our local area. The occupiers of the house were of a different nationality to me and the crew. Once the fire was extinguished they informed me that they poured the ashes from a BBQ into the wheelie bin which had melted the plastic and set fire to the contents of the bin

My considerations were to ensure that they were safe and that they understood fully the community safety message I was trying to communicate to them. I fully appreciated how vulnerable they must have been feeling so I took extra time to help them. I soon realised that the occupiers were struggling to understand the message I was providing them with.

I started off by sitting them down and reassured them that I fully understood their concerns. I removed the language barrier by carefully explaining where to put the ashes and what to do with them. I then provided a practical demonstration to reaffirm my message. Before we left the scene I confirmed with them that they understood the message and that they were happy with my actions.

COMMITMENT TO DEVELOPMENT

COMMITMENT TO DEVELOPMENT EXAMPLE

Describe a situation when you identified that your skills or the skills and knowledge of others needed to improve: What was the situation? What actions did you take? What was the outcome?

Whilst studying Advanced level in Media I had to create and produce a music video in a short timeframe. The pressure for me was operating unfamiliar, sophisticated and professional software called 'Final Cut'. This project would determine the outcome of my final grade and whether I would enter university.

To gain an understanding of the software I decided to set goals which would lead to successful completion of the project. Due to the time constraints I decided to stay after class up to 7pm on most days. Some evenings I had sessions with the college technician when I was struggling; especially for one session when the video I had filmed was not importing onto the computer. I asked for advice from the technician and learnt from his guidance and tuition. After I had finished I started a focus group to further improve my skills. I handed out a questionnaire for feedback on which parts of my video were good and which needed more work.

I completed the task with a new understanding of the software and was awarded with 'B' grade which helped significantly into getting conditional offers for my chosen universities.

COMMITMENT TO DEVELOPMENT EXAMPLE

Describe a situation when you identified that your skills or the skills and knowledge of others needed to improve: What was the situation? What actions did you take? What was the outcome?

I was in my first year at University and was given feedback on my essay writing. Although the feedback stated that my grades were acceptable, I was told that I would need to read more books to strengthen my argument and to show a clearer understanding of a subject. I identified the need to develop my skills in areas I was not doing well in, so I could achieve standards to the best of my ability.

I arranged a meeting with my tutor to discuss how I could improve my essay writing and what steps I would have to take to get better grades. I sought advice from my tutor as I knew I would benefit greatly from his knowledge and experience. Having being told to read a large range of books before starting to write my essays, I practiced different methods of essay writing and came up with a very effective method.

My grades improved dramatically and my tutor acknowledged my improvement in feedback. I have since advised a lot of friends and family who are at university with my method of writing essays.

COMMITMENT TO DEVELOPMENT EXAMPLE

Describe a situation when you identified that your skills or the skills and knowledge of others needed to improve: What was the situation? What actions did you take? What was the outcome?

Prior to my experience as a trainee volunteer firefighter, I felt that I needed to learn more about investigations into aircraft accidents to assist the Air Accident Investigations Branch with their enquires.

I enrolled on a home study course in Forensic Science as this involved learning and understanding crime scene investigations, murder investigations and fire investigations, all of which may be used when investigating aircraft incidents. I have now passed each stage of this course and have achieved a level three diploma.

The Forensic Science course has proven to be very useful as it has helped me with my firefighter training within the aviation environment and has also given me a greater depth of understanding on what is involved in various investigations involved after an incident.

COMMITMENT TO DEVELOPMENT EXAMPLE

Describe a situation when you identified that your skills or the skills and knowledge of others needed to improve: What was the situation? What actions did you take? What was the outcome?

During one of my first drill practice the station officer mentioned that we would be using the portable pump in training the following week. I identified that my skills and knowledge needed to improve on the portable pump as I had only used it on a recruit course and was worried about using it on a call.

The actions I took were to ask an experienced colleague if he would go over using the pump with me as soon as possible to improve my use and knowledge of the pump. My colleague was happy to help me and we worked together over the next three days until I was completely comfortable with using the pump. He revised priming the pump, what priming the pump does and the venturi effect. I listened to his feedback and implemented the training that he had provided.

The outcome of this was apparent shortly after, as we spent many days working at a dump fire. My revision paid off as I was completely confident and competent with using the portable pump at the call. Immediately after this incident I reviewed my performance against the operating procedures to confirm my competence levels.

COMMITMENT TO DEVELOPMENT EXAMPLE

Describe a situation when you identified that your skills or the skills and knowledge of others needed to improve: What was the situation? What actions did you take? What was the outcome?

Last year I attended a team meeting with my fellow engineers which was conducted by my field manager. During the meeting my manager asked if there was an engineer who would like to become a "laptop super user". This would be someone who had knowledge of the laptops and programs the company used and who would be able to resolve any technical issues an engineer has in the field or deliver training on new software/programs etc. when needed.

I felt that I lacked some of the technical knowledge required for the job but decided to volunteer my services and was offered the position.

I asked my manager whether there were any training I could undertake to enhance my skills and knowledge and was told I could attend several courses organised by British Gas to gain technical experience in the use of the laptop and its programs.

I also decided to contact super users in other local teams to ask for advice and knowledge of being a super user.

I have now successfully delivered several laptop induction courses to groups of new starters within the company and presented technical update briefings within my own team and have received positive feedback.

CONFIDENCE AND RESILIENCE

CONFIDENCE AND RESILIENCE EXAMPLE

Describe a time when, despite working in a challenging situation, you ensured you met your objectives: What was the situation? What challenges did you face? What actions did you take?

I was volunteering on a house building project in Costa Rica, building a house for a local under privileged family. On the site there were five other volunteers and three local labourers.

The first day was challenging as the labourers spoke little English and I had little knowledge in construction and felt out of my comfort zone. The constant poor communication made the environment stressful, challenging and potentially dangerous. There was a further challenge as we were working towards a tight deadline.

I remained calm and in control of my emotions. I took out my language dictionary and started translating words that would help me to communicate with the others. I then asked the volunteers what type of tasks they had been doing and if they could show me. With my notes I managed to translate the tasks and gain confidence by communicating effectively with the other members. I was able to show one labourer some health and safety issues as well as more efficient ways of carrying out tasks. I also utilised a fellow volunteer in helping to translate the labourer which allowed me to prepare for other tasks in advance.

CONFIDENCE AND RESILIENCE EXAMPLE

Describe a time when, despite working in a challenging situation, you ensured you met your objectives: What was the situation? What challenges did you face? What actions did you take?

During my final year at University, I had tight deadlines over the course of January. During this month, three essays and two big presentations were due in. I had planned in good time to complete half of this work over the Christmas holidays, however I had caught very bad flu so was falling behind with my work.

My Dyslexia had previously caused difficulty in working at a very quick pace and I knew what work ethic was required to hand in all my work on time. I knew that this work would count for a lot towards my final grade so I wanted to make sure that it was still up to a very high standard, despite the time restriction.

I wrote down all the work that was due in that month and the hand in dates, planning to work on more than one piece of work daily, as the deadlines were very close together. I was able to work out a schedule for how many hours I would spend on each piece of work so I could successfully hand them in on time. My hard work, focus and commitment meant all the work was handed in on time.

CONFIDENCE AND RESILIENCE EXAMPLE

Describe a time when, despite working in a challenging situation, you ensured you met your objectives: What was the situation? What challenges did you face? What actions did you take?

I was on duty at an air show as part of the St John Ambulance team. A report came in that a man had collapsed with a suspected heart attack and was gravely ill. Something needed to be done as quickly as possible.

My role in this was as operational assistant in the control unit. I was there with one other person who was in charge of the radio. I had to help coordinate the operation to help the emergency services, by relaying appropriate information via the radio operator and maintaining a clear log sheet record of the incident so the ambulance crews had clear information about the situation.

The ambulance promptly and paramedics were able to take the necessary action to save the man's life. The St John paramedic and my superintendent complimented me on the accuracy of my record keeping on the log sheet.

CONFIDENCE AND RESILIENCE EXAMPLE

Describe a time when, despite working in a challenging situation, you ensured you met your objectives: What was the situation? What challenges did you face? What actions did you take?

At one of my first Road Traffic Accidents when we arrived on scene, I noticed that the car was on its side with the casualty trapped inside. I was instructed by my sub-officer to stabilise the car.

I had only done this on my recruit course, had never completed it alone before and was very conscious of the casualty inside. However, we were short staffed this night and I had to be confident and complete it to the best of my ability. It was challenging as I had to operate complex equipment in a fast changing and life threatening situation. The actions I took to stabilise the car involved getting the ladder and ratchet straps from the appliance.

I then propped the car, under the wheels, at both ends with the ladder. I ran the ratchet straps through the wheels and around the ladder at both ends to secure the stability of the car. Despite doing this alone for the first time I completed the task efficiently and promptly. After the call I was surprised when my colleagues commended me on the job I did. I was glad I had done the job well and helped my team.

CONFIDENCE AND RESILIENCE EXAMPLE

Describe a time when, despite working in a challenging situation, you ensured you met your objectives: What was the situation? What challenges did you face? What actions did you take?

Whilst working as an electrician for British Gas, I attended a call at a property. Upon arriving I was greeted by a lady customer who appeared to be intoxicated. The lady in question was, however, calm and I proceeded with the repair.

During the repair, the lady demanded that all of the light switches in the property be changed as they were dated and she did not like them. I explained that this would be at an additional cost as her contract only covered repairs and not upgrades of fixtures and fittings. At this point she became aggressive and verbally abusive.

The challenges that I faced were that the customer was intoxicated and her behaviour may become unpredictable or threatening. I was aware that I needed to be sensitive in the dialogue that I had with the customer otherwise the situation could have rapidly deteriorated.

I responded to this challenging situation in a calm, confident and restrained way, telling the customer that I would listen to everything she had to say and building a rapport with her whilst concentrating on carrying out a professional repair and remaining in control of my own emotions.

OPENNESS TO CHANGE

OPENNESS TO CHANGE EXAMPLE

Describe a situation when you had to change the way you carry out a task because of an unexpected change in circumstances: What was the situation? What was your initial reaction to the change? How did you adapt to ensure you completed the task?

My colleges and I were called into a meeting. Our manager wanted to discuss ways in which the store could reduce cost but still provide a high quality and efficient service, so she announced that our replenishment team would have to work nights for a few months.

My initial reaction to the change was positive. I understood that the change was essential if the organisation was to continually improve. I felt it was part of my responsibility to embrace it. Although the change would impact significantly on my working patterns and my family, I wanted to do all I could to support the change.

In order to prepare for the change I discussed with the current night staff for advice on how to prepare for working unsociable hours and for new techniques of working. This enabled me to fully understand my new job role. I took their advice and re-arranged my other commitments including my studies, social time, gym training and sleeping patterns to improve productivity and allow the new working rota. I also adapted to their techniques and became more efficient, as well as becoming a more effective team member.

OPENNESS TO CHANGE EXAMPLE

Describe a situation when you had to change the way you carry out a task because of an unexpected change in circumstances: What was the situation? What was your initial reaction to the change? How did you adapt to ensure you completed the task?

We had a new General Manager at a restaurant who wanted to implement changes to how we shut down the establishment after work. This included labelling all fruit and juices, wiping all spirt bottles and cleaning underneath the drinks glasses on a nightly basis. Most of these tasks were previously done weekly, and doing them on a nightly basis would take more time at the end of each shift.

I accepted and supported these changes and knew that they were necessary to achieve high standards in the work place. I supported my General Manager's decision, despite resentment from some of the other workers. I encouraged my colleagues to have pride in the place they were working and welcomed these changes so the establishment could achieve its highest potential.

I would seek advice from my General Manager for how long I should date chopped fruit for which did not have a sell by date. I also requested more pens on the bar, so we were all able to label the fruit. For the first week I would ask my General Manager to check how our shut down was at the end of each shift, to make sure it was done correctly.

OPENNESS TO CHANGE EXAMPLE

Describe a situation when you had to change the way you carry out a task because of an unexpected change in circumstances: What was the situation? What was your initial reaction to the change? How did you adapt to ensure you completed the task?

In my laboratory work, large bottles of water were being put through a sterilization process which included rapid heating. Following a incident involving an explosion that caused the bottles to shatter in the process, it was decided by senior staff and the engineer that it was unsafe to put glassware of this size through sterilization.

I had to implement a change in procedure to establish a safer way of dealing with the situation so that when putting glassware through a sterilization process, which was to check that there were no large bottles in the discard boxes before being loaded into the machines.

As a result of this change, the work environment was made safer. I was very happy to implement the change as I would be for any change that made for efficient working practice and more than happy to discuss any issues with management.

OPENNESS TO CHANGE EXAMPLE

Describe a situation when you had to change the way you carry out a task because of an unexpected change in circumstances: What was the situation? What was your initial reaction to the change? How did you adapt to ensure you completed the task?

I worked as a Carpenter for six years. Over the six years I gained a lot of experience and worked on a wide variety of jobs, including roofing, first fixing and second fixing. Most of the work I did during my apprenticeship was on block built houses. After a few years there was a shift towards timber frame houses in the construction industry. This was a challenge to me as I had not trained in this area. My initial reaction to the change was positive. I believe change has many positive effects and it was my intention to embrace it. I researched erecting timber frame houses and soon realised that that I had the required skills from other jobs and training I had done. I enjoyed the learning process and increasing my expertise as a carpenter. Although I was working independently on many jobs at this stage of my apprenticeship, my boss acted as my mentor on the first job. I ensured that I accomplished this new task by working cooperatively with my team, following the instructions of my boss, learning as much as I could and completing the job to the highest standard.

OPENNESS TO CHANGE

Describe a situation when you had to change the way you carry out a task because of an unexpected change in circumstances: What was the situation? What was your initial reaction to the change? How did you adapt to ensure you completed the task?

Several months ago I was asked to travel down to Wales to be part of a team carrying out installation of solar panels. Electrical regulations stipulate that any new circuit installed in a property must be protected by an RCD. Having checked the installation we found that the existing fuse box inside the property was protected by an RCD fitted outside of the house at the electric meter. We commenced work and several hours later I received a call from a British Gas safety engineer who informed us that it was now British Gas policy to install a new fuse box with internal RCD in these circumstances.

I immediately accepted the change in policy and explained the situation and the need for a fuse box change to my colleagues.

Having almost completed the installation of the circuit I liaised with my colleagues and discussed how we could change the fuse box and complete the testing promptly and accurately without over-running the job extensively and causing inconvenience to the customer. We planned a new course of action and my team-mate installed the new fuse box while another colleague and I worked together to complete and test the installation effectively.

FINAL TIPS FOR COMPLETING A SUCCESSFUL APPLICATION FORM

Whilst some of the following tips have already been provided within this section, it is important that we provide them again. Your success very much depends on your ability to do the following:

- Read the application form and the guidance notes at least twice before you complete it.
- If possible, photocopy the application form and complete a draft copy first. This will allow you to make any errors or mistakes without being penalised.
- Obtain a copy of the core competencies and have them at your side when completing the form.
- Take your time when completing the form and set aside plenty of time for each question. I recommend that you spend 5 evenings completing the application form breaking it down into manageable portions. This will allow you to maintain high levels of concentration.
- Complete the form in the correct colour ink and follow all instructions very carefully. Your form could be thrown out for simply failing to follow simple instructions.

- Be honest when completing the form and if you are unsure about anything contact the police force for confirmation.
- Try not to make any spelling or grammar errors. You WILL lose marks for poor spelling, grammar and punctuation.
- Try to use keywords and phrases in your responses to the assessable questions that are relevant to the core competencies.
- Get someone to check over your form for errors before you submit it. If they can't read your application form, the assessor probably won't be able to either.
- Take a photocopy of your final completed form before submitting it.
- Try to submit the form well before the closing date. Some forces may operate a cut-off point in terms of the number of applications they receive.
- Some forms do get lost in the post so it is advisable that you send it by recorded delivery for peace of mind.
- If your form is unsuccessful ask for feedback, if available. It is important that you learn from your mistakes.

Printed in Great Britain
by Amazon